Satan's Four Stations:

The Destroyer is Destroyed

Books by Paul J. Bucknell

Allowing the Bible to speak to our lives today!

- Overcoming Anxiety: Finding Peace, Discovering God
- Reaching Beyond Mediocrity: Being an Overcomer
- The Life Core: Discovering the Heart of Great Training
- The Godly Man: When God Touches a Man's Life
- Redemption Through the Scriptures
- Godly Beginnings for the Family
- Principles and Practices of Biblical Parenting
- Building a Great Marriage
- Christian Premarital Counseling Manual for Counselors
- Relational Discipleship: Cross Training
- Running the Race: Overcoming Lusts
- Book of Genesis: The Bible Teaching Commentary
- Book of Romans: The Bible Teaching Commentary
- Book of Romans: Bible Studies
- Book of Ephesians: Bible Studies
- Walking with Jesus: Abiding in Christ
- Inductive Bible Studies in Titus
- 1 Peter Bible Study Questions: Living in a Fallen World
- Satan's Four Stations: The Destroyer is Destroyed
- Take Your Next Step into Ministry
- The Lord Your Healer
- Training Leaders for Ministry
- Study Guide for Jonah: Understanding God's Heart

➡ Check out our digital libraries at
www.foundationsforfreedom.net

Satan's Four Stations:

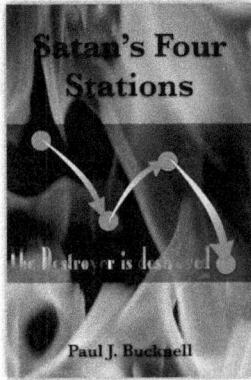

The Destroyer is Destroyed

Paul J. Bucknell

Satan's Four Stations: The Destroyer is Destroyed

Copyright ©2015 Paul J. Bucknell

Paperback:

ISBN-10: 1-61993-069-2

ISBN-13: 978-1-61993-069-8

Digital book formats:

ISBN-10: 1-61993-061-7

ISBN-13: 978-1-61993-061-2

www.foundationsforfreedom.net
info@foundationsforfreedom.net

Pittsburgh, PA 15212 USA

An Outline of Satan's Fall

4 Stages of Satan
Seen in Revelation

Satan's Four Stations: An Introduction

As Seen in the Book of Revelation

The Book of Revelation has an astounding way of presenting the gospel and other behind-the-scenes information on topics like Satan–the devil, even though this knowledge is generally stated in other scripture passages.

While preparing for teaching a class on Revelation 9, I noticed the numerous times Satan was referred to and thought that it was crucial to gain a complete picture of who the devil is and how he extends his authority. Satan is the Destroyer, ruining things as much as he is able.

This study is largely limited to the Book of Revelation, though some scriptural cross-referencing is provided to clarify, strengthen, and complete this study.

There are the four stations or stages of Satan as seen in the Book of Revelation: (1) From Heaven, (2) In the Abyss, (3) Released from the Abyss, and finally (4) In the Lake of Fire, each greatly influencing his powers and ability to deceive.

1. From Heaven (Rev 9:1; 12:9)

Satan's Origin

9:1 And the fifth angel sounded, and I saw a **star from heaven** which had fallen to the earth; and the key of the bottomless pit was given to **him**.

12:9 And the **great dragon** was thrown down, the **serpent of old who is called the devil and Satan**, ...was thrown down to (lit. into) the earth, and his angels...

> *"A star from heaven which had fallen."*
> *"Was thrown down...into the earth."*

Satan's Original Station

There is no question as to whether the devil is a real person or not. Satan is not just a representation of evil power but an instigator of wickedness. The more important question concerns Satan's origin. Where did he come from? He clearly was not eternal, so did God make him? If so, why would the Lord make the evil one and allow all the suffering instigated by Satan's hand? Some of these deeper questions might not be fully answered in Revelation, but the scriptural references supply basic observations from which insightful answers can be deducted.

The two passages listed above give evidence of the evil one's former 'residence' to be in heaven alongside God Himself. Satan was a star (or like a star) fallen from heaven (9:1). "He was thrown down" (12:9) doubtlessly from heaven where God dwells. Both

Isaiah 14 and Ezekiel 28 affirm this interpretation and provide further interesting descriptions and reasons for his fall. Those that aligned themselves with Satan were also thrown down along with the evil one, "And his tail swept away a third of the stars of heaven, and threw them to the earth" (12:4).[1] Satan, then, has been forced out and thrown down out of heaven into the earth.

We should note that it is possible that this casting out took place in two stages, the first to be removed out of heaven (God's presence) and then cast to the earth. Are Ezekiel 28 and Isaiah 14 speaking prophetically of this casting down to the earth due to Christ's coming or is it referring to a former event–having been cast out, where he simply lost more control? Isaiah 14:12 speaks of Satan as already haven fallen and then a prophecy for the future in verse 15, "Nevertheless you will be thrust down to Sheol, to the recesses of the pit" (Is 14:15).

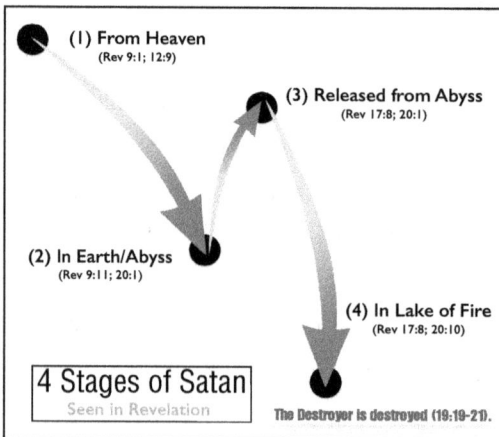

(1) From Heaven
(Rev 9:1; 12:9)

(3) Released from Abyss
(Rev 17:8; 20:1)

(2) In Earth/Abyss
(Rev 9:11; 20:1)

(4) In Lake of Fire
(Rev 17:8; 20:10)

4 Stages of Satan
Seen in Revelation

The Destroyer is destroyed (19:19-21).

The Timing of Satan Being Kicked Out

The Book of Revelation has not stressed the specifics of when the great dragon was kicked out of heaven, but as we refer back to the Gospels, we

---

[1] Stars refer to heavenly objects including angels, Satan (9:1) and fallen angels (12:4) once in God's presence. It is said of Satan, "But you said in your heart, 'I will ascend to heaven; I will raise my throne above the stars of God" (Isa 14:13). The rebellious stars stationed high in heaven were cast down. We are not sure of any meaning beyond that.

find Jesus spoke quite clearly about Satan's fall which was tied to Jesus' first coming, the casting out of demons becoming a visible sign that the devil had lost his former position.

> And the seventy returned with joy, saying, "Lord, even the demons are subject to us in Your name." [18] And He said to them, "**I was watching Satan fall from heaven like lightning**. [19] Behold, I have given you authority to tread upon serpents and scorpions, and over all the power of the enemy, and nothing shall injure you.[20] Nevertheless do not rejoice in this, that the spirits are subject to you, but rejoice that your names are recorded in heaven" (Lu 10:17-20).

Satan's New Destination

Verse 9:1 states that Satan was given the key[2] to the bottomless pit which became his new temporary 'office' location.[3] The word 'given' reminds us Satan only possesses delegated authority as Christ has the final authority of death and Hades (1:18).

Satan was formerly a star–a great angel of heaven but because of his pride was cast out. Some of his other names are the devil, destroyer and accuser. Satan did not fall alone but many of the angels fell with him to carry out his work (Jude 6). These 'fallen stars' are what we call demons, evil spirits or devils, angels who were cast out of heaven because of their disloyalty to God and His purposes.

---

[2] Mounce argues against the angel falling from heaven as being Satan but rather alludes to another divine agent that "descends" to do God's biding, probably the same as in 20:1 (*The Book of Revelation* by Robert Mounce, p. 192-193).

[3] It is obvious that though Satan is given the key here, because Christ is said to hold it in 1:18 and an angel in 20:1, it is only temporary. But with possession of it, Satan is willing to do his worse with the authority that he has.

Verses 12:7-9 confirms the abyss to be Satan's new holding place as 9:1 and 20:1 states, but it is not at first obvious because the scripture is often translated "to the earth" which would appear to be on the earth's surface. The preposition, however, literally uses "into" (Greek: *eis*) rather than "to" which indicates that he was not running about on earth but finds habitation in the abyss from which he hatches his operations (9:1-11).

The abyss certainly could be a figurative rather than physical place in the center of the earth, but the place is real and so is Satan's containment. Whether its location be in the physical or spiritual realm is hard to be certain.

Conclusion

Satan is very powerful and still retains much authority although always under God's jurisdiction. The Dragon was not immediately and finally judged as is evident but allowed to reveal his corrupt nature by his deeds throughout earth's history, starting in Genesis 3 and 4, continuing on throughout the Old Testament age, on earth during Jesus' life (i.e. betrayal Lu 22:3), during the growth of the church (12:17), and right to his demise which is later powerfully but succinctly described in Revelation 20.

Discussion Study Questions

1. Why might Satan formerly be called a star (9:1)? What was his name before he fell (Is 14:12; note KJV's translation of this verse)?

2. For what reason was Satan cast from heaven (Isaiah 14 and Ezekiel 28)?

3. What is the difference between Jesus, God's Son, being sent to earth and Satan being cast out of heaven?

4. What does Jesus' observation in Luke 10:17-18 further reveal about the evil one?

2. In the Earth/Abyss (Rev 9:11; 20:1-3)

Satan's Limitations

9:11 They have as king over them, the angel of the abyss; his name in Hebrew is Abaddon, and in the Greek.

20:1-3 And I saw an angel coming down from heaven, having the key of the abyss and a great chain in his hand... 3 and threw him into the abyss, and shut it and sealed it over him, so that he should not deceive the nations any longer.

Satan

(1) From Heaven (Rev 9:1; 12:9; Lu 10:17-18; Is 14:12-14)

9:1 And the fifth angel sounded, and I saw a star from heaven which had fallen to the earth; and the key of the bottomless pit was given to him.

12:9 And the great dragon was thrown down, the serpent of old who is called the devil and Satan, ... was thrown down into the earth, and his angels...

(2) In Earth/Abyss (Rev 9:11; 20:1)

9:11 They have as king over them, the angel of the abyss; his name in Hebrew is Abaddon, and in the Greek.

20:1 And I saw an angel coming down from heaven, having the key of the abyss and a great chain in his hand... 3 and threw him into the abyss, and sealed it over him, so that he should not deceive the nations any longer.

"The angel of the abyss"
"Threw him into the abyss"

The question of where Satan was thrown and what he is doing, then, becomes of great interest due to his ongoing power and influence on individuals, false prophets and beasts (i.e. governments) here on earth.

In the Lord's prayer Jesus trains His disciples to pray, "Deliver us from the evil one" (Mat 6:13).[4] We need to gain protection from Satan's treacherous purposes for he purposes to bring harm to many–as is clearly seen from Revelation 1 onwards–and ultimately becomes the reason for the destruction of the contaminated heaven and earth (2 Pe 3:10).

The Book of Job also shows the intensity with which Satan pursues others with destruction. Satan's same passion to gain control is evident wherever he appears. For this reason we must make special precaution not to get preoccupied with the dead, death or violence as is popular with some.

Most people assume that the evil one rules over the earth. These views can be somewhat legitimized by the way the evil one brings his disastrous touch to the people on the earth.

> "In which you formerly walked according to the course of this world, according to the prince of the power of the air, of the spirit that is now working in the sons of disobedience" (Eph 2:2).

> "Be of sober spirit, be on the alert. Your adversary, the devil, prowls about like a roaring lion, seeking someone to devour" (1 Pet 5:8).

We are hardly denying Satan's cunning ability to presently deceive and trouble God's people, retain control of unbelievers (John 8:44) or even to persecute believers (2:13) but are honestly trying to understand the implications of   what it means when it says that Satan fell from heaven. The evil one's corrupted and deceived heart leads him to use whatever power he has to deceive the world

---

[4] "Evil one" in the Lord's prayer is a better translation than an impersonal "evil".

to worship him which becomes one of the main anti-themes outlined in the *Book of Revelation*. When he breathes, smokes pours forth accompanied by terrible objects. But let us look a bit more carefully at Satan's holding place. Where does he rule from?

Verse 9:11 mocks the evil one by describing the abyss as his kingdom. He is king over the abyss which is completely opposite to Christ's throne in chapters 4-5. Satan's kingdom is 'expansive' in that it is bottomless. The word 'abyss' is used numerous times in Revelation (Rev 11:7; 17:8; 20:1,3) and is sometimes translated as bottomless, unbounded, abyss or of "Orcus, a very deep gulf or chasm in the lowest parts of the earth used as the common receptacle of the dead and especially as the abode of demons."[5]

This dark, desperate place is a far cry from his former dwelling place where bright lights and the glory of heaven emanate from God's presence. Now away from God's presence, Satan hides in the darkness of the abyss with his hideous patrons away from God's presence, "For He delivered us from the domain of darkness, and transferred us to the kingdom of His beloved Son" (Col 1:13). Satan exercises his limited power from his allotted dark closet.

Some might object that Rev 9:1 and 12:9 both say that Satan was cast down to the earth rather than the abyss. First, we need to consider that the scripture clearly states that the devil ends up in the abyss, "They have as king over them, the angel of the abyss" (12:9). Second, we need to remind ourselves that the literal reading is not "to the earth" but "into the earth" which actually affirms the thought that the evil one was cast into the abyss, thought of as the center of the earth rather than on the earth.

---

[5] *Thayer's Greek-English Lexicon of the New Testament* from Online Bible.

The Timing

Revelation 20 is a hotly disputed passage, but as stated above, these verses only confirm Satan's presently limited powers and that his control room is in the abyss. John describes what had happened, "Threw him into the abyss" (Rev 20:1). The debate is not whether he ever goes into the abyss but the timing of this event. While there, he has only limited powers.

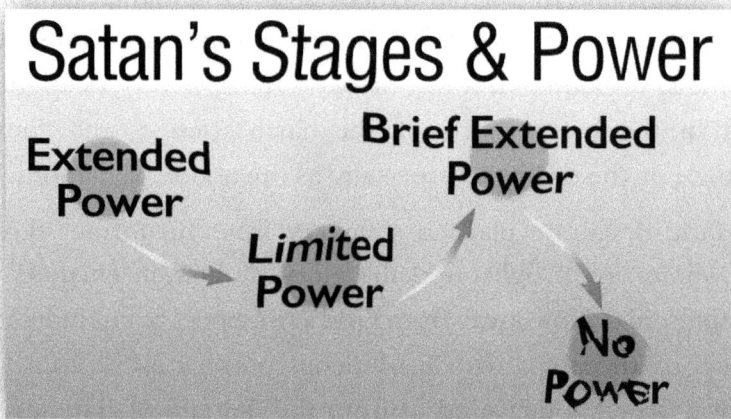

The thousand years of Revelation 20 depicts the binding of the evil one for a long, undetermined period, being greatly limited in the use of his power. His lost of position is directly related to his restrained powers and this is a perfect match of the current church age–Satan is greatly limited in the evil he wants to do. Look how Jesus' powers and those passed on to His disciples depict Satan's limited power.

> "But if I cast out demons by the Spirit of God, then the kingdom of God has come upon you. Or how can anyone enter the strong man's house and carry off his property,

unless he first binds the strong man? And then he will plunder his house" (Mat 12:28-29).

At the end just preceding Satan's full judgment, he will be released, enabling him to expand his delusive powers and bring great destructive control over the earth. As he is allowed to exercise his deceptive power, we get to see his real nature and ultimate purposes of self-worship and self-adoration, making quite apparent that his coming judgment is just and fitting. This is exactly what we find in the passages throughout Revelation—persecution followed by great delusion and the masses of unrepentant and hardened soldiers of Satan. Only then is Satan and others judged.

Some people see this 1000 years as a literal future 1000 years of peace and apparently believe Satan has absolutely no power during that age,[6] but many pieces do not fit neatly together when this picture is adopted. It is much more consistent and cohesive to accept Jesus' interpretation of Satan's presently limited powers due to the devil's binding linked to our present time, especially as Satan's limitations are directly related to the Gospel outreach to the nations as specified in the text, "So that he should not deceive the nations any longer, until the thousand years were completed; after these things he must be released for a short time" (Rev 20:3).

The main focus in the Book of Revelation is the unveiling of God's grand redemption purpose held in the scroll (some translations call it a book) (chapter 5; 10:8-11). We suggest this 'throwing down' to the abyss happened during Jesus' first coming: His life, ministry, death, resurrection and ascension.

---

[6] I have presented my arguments that the millennium refers to the church age in my study on Rev 20, the millennium (found in BFF's NT Digital Library).

What are we to conclude from Jesus' words? Clearly, Satan is somehow limited in power, at least as far as it has to do with the disciples doing miracles, casting out demons and going about preaching the gospel. Satan's "fall" then is related to the ability of the gospel to spread throughout the world, that is, the various nations. Satan's ability to hinder the light from shining is drastically cut back. When challenged, he must back down. Note the confidence of the saints, "Therefore, take up the full armor of God, that you may be able to resist in the evil day, and having done everything, to stand firm" (Eph 6:13).

Nor is it only Jesus who can cast out demons, but His disciples too. Although Jesus' disciples and apostles went forth to the nations, we should not for a moment conclude that Satan has lost his ability to frustrate the advance of the gospel. The dragon repeatedly attempts to hinder the spread of the Gospel. The Book of Acts records many such incidents: "You who are full of all deceit and fraud, you son of the devil" (Ac 13:11). And although the Book of Acts ends with Paul the Apostle in prison, we see the Gospel released to the nations, "Preaching the kingdom of God, and teaching concerning the Lord Jesus Christ **with all openness, unhindered**" (Acts 28:31).

If we can accept (and we should) there is some restriction of Satan's power during this present age, then it likely described by this binding in Revelation 20:1-3. The devil is limited in power during our present age so that the gospel can go forth to the nations. Satan's limit of power is associated with his fall. If we assume Satan is not now restricted in his power, are we prepared to assert that Satan now has full use of his powers (as in the final tribulation)? I think not.

There is another point that must be carefully noticed. Rev 20:3 associates the release of the evil one with increased deception of the nations, "And will come out to deceive the nations which are in the four corners of the earth, Gog and Magog, to gather them together for the war; the number of them is like the sand of the seashore" (Rev 20:8). Does this not bring to one's mind the escalation of evil pointed to earlier in the Book of Revelation (chapter 9, etc.)? As Revelation unfolds its secrets, a delusion of the nations takes place, implying that the devil has been released and increased his power over the nations.

> "And he said to me, 'The waters which you saw where the harlot sits, are peoples and multitudes and nations and tongues'" (Re 17:15).

> "For all the nations have drunk of the wine of the passion of her immorality" (18:3).

> "And this gospel of the kingdom shall be preached in the whole world for a witness to all the nations, and then the end shall come" (Mat 24:14).

In Matthew 24:14 Jesus clearly ties the gospel being preached to the nations as one of the key markers of the end of the age. If we assume Satan is not restricted of his power now, then how does the Gospel spread to the nations? This probably is what is meant by the sealing of the 144,000 must first happen (Rev 7:3-4; 14:1-3) for otherwise the believers would be deluded themselves and give their allegiance to the devil. The "sealing" must first take place where the elect are secured. Once this point is reached, it will lead us to the next step when the evil one is released. If we think Satan's power is terrible now, what will happen when he is released? Let's look at these things in Satan's next position.

Conclusion

Satan was thrown down out of heaven into the abyss and suffers limitations on hindering the Gospel from going out to the nations. Jesus and His kingdom are growing greatly and therefore could cast out Legion (so named because there were many) of demons from the mad man and send them into the herd of swine (Mark 5:8-15). At the very end of the age Satan will gain more power to deceive the nations, but that is when he is released from the Abyss, bringing about a great persecution against God's people. This full display of power is not yet present. The 1000 years. the millennium, is better understood as the church age where Satan's powers are limited by God's people.

Discussion Study Questions

1. Where is Satan thrown from and to? How do you know?

2. Do you believe Satan can fully utilize his power in the present? Present the reasons for your answer.

3. Make a contrast between Satan and Christ Jesus from the Book of Revelation including their habitation, purpose and names.

3. Released from Abyss (Rev 17:8; 20:1)

Satan's Release

11:7 And when they have finished their testimony, the beast that comes up out of the abyss will make war with them, and overcome them and kill them.

17:8 The beast that you saw was and is not, and is about to come up out of the abyss...

20:1 He must be released for a short time.

> *"The beast that comes up out of the abyss will make war"*
> *"He must be released for a short time."*

Several places in Revelation very forcefully state that Satan **must be** released from being restrained in the abyss. There are several parallels here: the repeated "out of the abyss" description indicates increased control and authority while the phrase "for a short time" describes its brief duration. His new position "out of abyss" is linked with increased powers which are definitely seen as we go through Revelation.

For example, in the verses above we find that the beast is said to come up out of the abyss. Every time an object ascends from the abyss something hideous appears with tragedy closely following behind. Just as God uses the heathen nations to bring judgment to others in the Old Testament (Hab 1:6), so He continues to use others such as the devil to bring judgment upon the unrepentant.

- Revelation 9:1-12 first uses the word 'abyss' (bottomless pit in NASB) with reckless locusts coming out along with the smoke from the abyss. In 9:11 we see that their king, evidently leading them, is the devil himself for his name is Destruction (Abaddon, Apollyon). Once the angel opened the pit, the smoke, representing the evil one and his horde, came forth (9:2).

- In chapter 11 we find the two witnesses, representing all of God's people, valiantly testifying of the gospel (c.f. 10:11) up to the time when the evil one is released when they can no longer openly spread God's truth. We ask, "How will Satan's power be any different once loosed?" This chapter reveals this answer by the phrase: "Will make war with them and will kill them" (11:7). The final days will see an increased opposition to those that openly believe and share the gospel, though some suggest this opposition is localized against the Jews and Christians in certain regions. The beast is symbolic of the evil one (11:7). Satan, the beast and the false prophet operate as one and will be destroyed together (20:10) (4th station).

- The seventh bowl in chapter 17 depicts the judgment of the wicked up to the final restoration of the sealed. In verse 17:8 the beast, representative of the evil one, again comes up out from the abyss. This is not another attack but the same picture from a different angle on how the evil one uses his short-lived power to curse those on the earth. Note how the non-sealed are described here: "Whose name has not been written in the book of life from the foundation of the world" (17:8; 20:15) which again shows the great delusion the evil one will cast over the world. Nations and governments will come together against the Lamb (17:14).

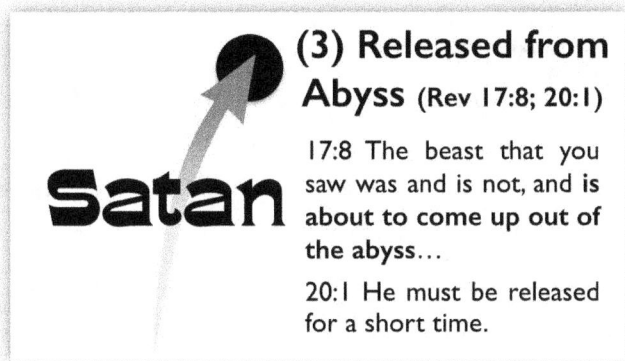

(3) Released from Abyss (Rev 17:8; 20:1)

17:8 The beast that you saw was and is not, and is about to come up out of the abyss...

20:1 He must be released for a short time.

- "He must be released for a short time" (20:1). This final description of the devil knits the former scenes together in a brief final description, linking the evil one with the short period in which all the final acts of destruction occur. He is the source of the devastating destruction.

Short time

This period of his release from the abyss is not only distinguished by a sudden increase of Satan's power but also its short duration. This again is noted throughout Revelation as it says in 20:1, "for a short time."

> "Woe to the earth and the sea, because the devil has come down to you, having great wrath, knowing that he has only a short time" (Rev 12:12).

The whole point of this temporary release of the evil one along with increased use of his powers is seen in the fact that it is short and temporary. "After these things he must be released for a short time" (Rev 20:3). He **must** be released, however. This is part of the prophetic plan–expected and planned for.

Destruction, Signs, Deceit

Satan's display of power was earlier contained and subdued, but now several terrible signs will come: great calamity–for he brings as much trouble as he can; powerful signs and wonders, and deceit–he controls by deception and manipulation.

> "And he performs great signs, so that he even makes fire come down out of heaven to the earth in the presence of men. [14] And he deceives those who dwell on the earth because of the signs which it was given him to perform in the presence of the beast, telling those who dwell on the earth to make an image to the beast who had the wound of the sword and has come to life" (Rev 13:13-14).

> "For they are spirits of demons, performing signs, which go out to the kings of the whole world, to gather them together for the war of the great day of God, the Almighty" (Rev 16:14).

> "And the beast was seized, and with him the false prophet who performed the signs in his presence" (Rev 19:20).

These verses bring out what happens when Satan performs extraordinary signs through the beast and false prophet. It appears this is much more than an advanced technological technique but, in any case, he uses his power to astonish many. The deception, however, goes hand in hand with his signs and wonders (perhaps even these wonders are part of his gimmick). This greatly contrasts with our Lord who limits His miraculous signs so that His people can learn to live by faith, but the evil one gorges himself on self-worship and only cares to seize the attention and worship of the multitudes.

A Summary from 2 Thessalonians 2

Satan's picture is first glimpsed at in the Old Testament, first as the serpent, daring to counter God's Word and deceiving Eve (Gen 3:4) but later in the prophets as a 'small horn' (Daniel 8:9-11; 7:25). The New Testament likewise speaks about increased deceptions, signs, coldness of heart, an age of sensuality connected to the personification of the evil one. 2 Thessalonians 2 does a great job of summarizing the end of the age which is closely linked to this third stage. Some people who read Revelation have a very difficult time associating it to the world in which we live, but Paul does a good job of this as Jesus did.

These things will happen but the timing is important. One misunderstanding comes through teaching the word "restrains" in 1 Th 2:7 refers to the church or the Holy Spirit that takes up the church.[7] Though some people insist that it is the church that is removed by rapture before the tribulation (i.e. 1 Th 4:16-17), 2 Thessalonians 2 connects "our gathering" with Christ's coming, "To the coming of our Lord Jesus Christ, and our gathering together to Him" (1 Th 2:1). Perhaps that which restrains is God who says He holds back the evil one until all His people are sealed

---

[7] "For the mystery of lawlessness is already at work; **only he who now restrains** will do so until he is taken out of the way" (1 Th 2:7).

(i.e. saved).[8] This is also confirmed by Jesus, "And this gospel of the kingdom shall be preached in the whole world for a witness to all the nations, and then the end shall come" (Mt 24:14).

> "And then that **lawless one will be revealed** whom the **Lord will slay** with the breath of His mouth and bring to an end **by the appearance of His coming**; [9] that is, the one whose coming is in accord with the activity of Satan, with all power and signs and false wonders, [10] and with all the deception of wickedness for those who perish, because they did not receive the love of the truth so as to be saved" (2 Th 2:8-10).

Paul here summarizes the final scenes of the world as we know it: (1) The revelation of the lawless one (personification of Satan), then (2) Great deception and wickedness, (3) God's destruction of the evil one, and (4) Jesus' coming. This is exactly what we find repeated many times throughout Revelation. Satan's "activity" will be revealed through the lawless one's "all power and signs and false wonders" combined with deception and wickedness.

Conclusion

Satan has been restrained so that the Gospel can go to the ends of the world, but we should not assume that this present period reveals Satan's full power of deception. Absolutely not. Satan will be released once the elect are sealed, and then he will bring the world under his deception through false signs. By admitting to a coming greater display of the evil one's power once the elect has

---

[8] It is the complete number of the chosen ones being saved that holds back the evil one's release, "When they have finished their testimony, the beast that comes up" (Rev 11:7). This is the same meaning as, "'Do not harm the earth or the sea or the trees, until we have sealed the bond-servants of our God on their foreheads.' And I heard the number of those who were sealed, one hundred and forty-four thousand sealed from every tribe of the sons of Israel" (Rev 7:3-4).

been secured, we verify that Satan is presently to some degree restrained, which again provides strong evidence that Satan is still 'bound' in the abyss but will soon be released for a short time.

One huge mistake is to assume the church will not go through tribulations. Another is to think what we now see is the worse of Satan's deception. Jesus, Paul, Peter and here John all warn us of worse times, and we need to prepare our souls by affirming our willingness to follow Jesus even if we need to die for Him.

Discussion Study Questions

1. Do you think Satan is fully displaying his power now? Explain.

2. What are the signs of the evil one? What will happen when he gets his way?

3. Why does Satan have to be released "for a short time" (Rev 20:1,3)?

4. Share three ways that you demonstrate that you personally love the truth.

4. In the Lake of Fire (Rev 17:8; 20:10)

Satan's Demise

17:8 The beast ... is about to come up out of the abyss and to go into destruction.

20:10 And the devil who deceived them was thrown into the lake of fire and brimstone... they will be tormented day and night forever and ever.

> ### *"And go into destruction"*
> ### *"The devil...was thrown into the lake of fire"*

John's way of writing verse 17:8 brings great comfort to believers for although he alludes to Satan's powerful spell of deception, his destruction will be swallowed up in a moment. In other words, Satan's rise of power is but for a short moment. Satan's final demise is near even before it begins. His judgment is set even before he is released from the abyss.

The unholy trinity: beast, false prophet and Satan will all be thrown into the lake of fire and be tormented forever (Rev 20:10). The description of the final judgment is clearly not annihilation but eternal perdition–suffering ongoing judgment with those who share his mark, "they will be tormented day and night forever and ever" (Rev 20:10, 14-15). The lawless one is called the "son of destruction" since he personifies Satan. This is completely in opposition to Jesus who is the Son of God who does His Father's will.

An Explanation

There are at least two reasons for the Lord to allow this great burst of wickedness and judgment. By allowing evil to grow, its innate evil and connection with the evil one is seen as just and deserved. For example, those having relatives killed in a terrorist bombing see firsthand the great evil plotted by the evil one and reflect justice by desiring revenge of the wicked plotters.

People in every age are convinced that they are good,

(4) In Lake of Fire
(Rev 17:8; 20:10)

17:8 The beast ... is about to come up out of the abyss and **to go into destruction.**

20:10 And the devil who deceived them was thrown into the lake of fire and brimstone... they will be tormented day and night forever and ever.

Satan

THE DESTROYER IS DESTROYED (19:19-21).

but in fact they are wicked. In order to reveal the genuine wickedness of the heart, all the props which God has established in the past to preserve morality: family, varying languages, and separation of cultures, all must be stripped away. When this societal support is knocked down as in Noah's time (Mt 24:37), Satan will waste little time to increase the spread of wickedness. When a person can become as wicked, deceptive and disruptive as he wants, selfishness rules, and the weak are oppressed.

Lawlessness[9] greatly differs from God's kingdom of love where people through the Holy Spirit[10] suppress their sinful inclinations and choose what is right and good, choosing to help those in need. But the wicked, when freed from former restraints of the world, gorge themselves on evil revealing the evil of their hearts.

There is yet another answer to these questions that runs deeper behind the scenes. These difficult questions easily pop up during times of judgment:

- Why does God allow evil?

- Why did God allow for the opportunity for sin in the garden?

These questions, derived from readers of Genesis, often reappear when reading Revelation but become further developed. For example, let's extend these same questions to the text of Rev 20:1,3 where it states, "He (Satan) must be released." Parallel questions easily develop.

- Why must Satan be released?

- Isn't it better to keep Satan bound and let the gospel keeping going forth?

These questions delve deep into theological issues. But their answers need not be difficult, though perhaps the answers are not the ones that we expect. God has created this world and allowed this vein of wickedness to further reveal His awesome person: His wrath, power and mercy. Revelation chapters 4-5 boldly display

---

[9] Terrorism is only one kind of lawlessness. Others include bribery, misleading facts, injustice, and plain immorality. Our age tunneling into increased perversity and deception surely could lead into the final stage of wickedness.

[10] All of us start with this innately evil heart and only by being born again, receiving a new heart of love from God, can we change (John 3).

that everything starts in the throne room and revolves around God's glory.[11]

> [8] And the four living creatures, each one of them having six wings, are full of eyes around and within; and day and night they do not cease to say, "Holy, holy, holy, is the Lord God, the Almighty, who was and who is and who is to come." [9] And when the living creatures give glory and honor and thanks to Him who sits on the throne, to Him who lives forever and ever, [10] the twenty-four elders will fall down before Him who sits on the throne, and will worship Him who lives forever and ever, and will cast their crowns before the throne..." (Rev 4:8-10).

God is all glorious, while the evil one along with everything else, stands wholly dependent upon God for their glory, purpose, and existence. While Satan once was beautiful, he sought out his purpose independent from the Lord and has become hideous apart from God's glory (this is why monsters are hideous). In the end, we cannot question the wisdom of God's design but accompany all the angels, creatures and elders declaring God's worth of <u>all</u> praise. We join with them in declaring the glory of God's special redemptive plan where the Lord gloriously radiates the glory of His great love and wrath. God through these many scenes powerfully combines the display of His wrath and mercy in the scroll containing His redemptive plan revealing His wisdom and power which otherwise would be tucked away (Rev 4-5).

> "[22] What if God, although willing to <u>demonstrate His wrath and to make His power</u> known, endured with much

---

[11] Hendrickson in his commentary of Revelation describes this scene to be a picture of the universe (*More Than Conquerors*, p.102).

patience vessels of wrath prepared for destruction? [23] And He did so in order that He might <u>make known the riches of His glory upon vessels of mercy</u>, which He prepared beforehand for glory" (Rom 9:22-23).

Conclusion

Everyone whose name is not in the Book of Life will find their disastrous end in the Lake of Fire along with Satan, this last station, where the flames will endlessly declare God's righteousness by their flaming judgment. But the same sight also reminds us of those who are undeservingly saved by God's lavish love seen by the suffering wounds of the Lamb, God's Son, dying in the place of sinners on the cross. God's amazing love and grace will dazzle in front of us for all eternity. After all, we all rightfully deserve to burn in that eternal fire, for we too have all come short of His bright glory (Rom 3:23). God's wrath vindicates His righteousness and displays His amazing mercy and love though the judgment.

Discussion Study Questions

1. How does the clearcut judgment of the evil one bring encouragement to believers?

2. Is hell the same as the lake of fire describe here in Revelation (Rev 19:20; 20:14,15; 21:8)?

3. What are the characteristics of the lake of fire?

4. Explain in the end where you will end up? Why?

5. Is your name in the book of life? How so?

Appendix 1: Video

A video accompanies this theme recording Paul, the author, teaching for five minutes explaining this topic.

vimeo.com/142142892 (Password is: nt)[12]

---

[12] Connect with Paul at info@foundationsforfreedom.net with any problems.

Appendix 2: Author's Information

Rev. Paul J. Bucknell teaches Christian leadership seminars around the world and has authored more than twenty books on topics including: Christian life, discipleship, godly living, biblical studies, call to ministry, marriage, parenting and anxiety. His blend of knowledge from different fields along with his deep care for training of God's people provide many new insights into this book. Paul and his wife, Linda, live in the USA and have eight children and three grandchildren. He is the founder and president of Biblical Foundations for Freedom, a web-based ministry that releases God's powerful, life-changing truths worldwide.

www.foundationsforfreedom.net

www.ingramcontent.com/pod-product-compliance
Lightning Source LLC
Chambersburg PA
CBHW060634030426
42337CB00018B/3363